the forbidden CITY

Author: **Susie Hodge**
Consultant: **Emma Reisz**

tick tock
MEDIA

Copyright © *ticktock* Entertainment Ltd 2005

First published in Great Britain in 2005 by *ticktock* Media Ltd.,

Unit 2, Orchard Business Centre, North Farm Road, Tunbridge Wells, Kent, TN2 3XF

We would like to thank: Alison Howard, Jenni Rainford and Elizabeth Wiggans for their help with this book.

ISBN 1 86007 600 9 PB

Printed in China

A CIP catalogue record for this book is available from the British Library.

Contents

WITHDRAWN FROM STOCK

Introduction

Deep in the centre of Beijing, in northern China, and behind a giant wall, is a huge cluster of exotic palaces – known as the Forbidden City. The City was originally also called 'Gu Gong', which means 'Imperial Palace' in Chinese, or 'Danei', which means the 'Great Within'. It was home to 24 emperors between 1420 and 1924. The Chinese people believed their emperors were chosen by God and so few people questioned their authority. Even today, without any emperors living there, the Forbidden City looks breathtakingly lavish.

Two bronze lion sculptures flank the entrance to one of the buildings at the Forbidden City. Lions were symbolically regarded as guardians by the Chinese.

ENORMOUS – BUT SECRET

Although no longer occupied by royalty, the Forbidden City remains a symbol of Chinese power and one of the greatest royal palaces in the world. It is made up of 800 buildings, including magnificent halls, libraries, theatres, temples, homes, storehouses and offices. It covers approximately 74 hectares or 720,000 square metres and is surrounded by 10-metre high walls and a 6-metre deep moat.

There are four unique and delicately structured corner towers overlooking the City. Generally, it was divided into two parts, the northern half, or the Outer Court where emperors executed their supreme power over the nation and the southern half, or the Inner Court, where they lived with their royal family. It is believed that it took about a million labourers and craftsmen to build the lavish City. From the beginning, it was called the Forbidden City because only the emperor and his family, their staff and those on official imperial business could enter – the general public were not allowed inside. Even ministers and most servants who worked there had only a limited knowledge of the City's layout – as few people had access to all areas, even if they lived there. The main gate, called the Gate of Great Purity, was only opened for an emperor or empress and many other parts, including paths, steps and certain rooms, were only for the emperor and empress to use. So, the city was kept secret from the people for 500 years.

Today the Forbidden City is the Palace Museum, containing many works of art and treasures.

FROM PRIVATE TO PUBLIC

Even though the majority of people living in China were poor, most thought that it was fair for the emperor to live in such luxury. This was because they believed that the emperor was the Son of Heaven, appointed by God to look after the people on Earth. The sumptuous Forbidden City was therefore considered the perfect location for a god on Earth to live. Today, the Forbidden City is a popular tourist destination – visited as much for its unique architectural styles and brilliant colours as for the museum full of treasures that currently lies within its great halls.

It wasn't until 1925 that the Forbidden City was reincarnated as the 'Imperial Palace Museum'. Many of the beautiful porcelain, jade, ivory, silk and precious-metal treasures on show at the museum are wartime loot or gifts that arrived at the Forbidden City when it was still an emperor's home. Appropriate then, that they should be on show today in the very same location.

The Forbidden City is surrounded by a moat, which is known as the Imperial River or the Outer Golden River.

CHAPTER 1

How it was built

T he construction of the Forbidden City began in 1406, in the fourth year of Emperor Yongle's reign and took 14 years to complete. Astronomers planned the city to align with the Pole Star, which they believed to be at the centre of heaven. Architects planned the emperor's home to meet all the conditions of Feng Shui, to work with the forces of nature, not against them.

A HOUSE FIT FOR A LEADER

Emperor Yongle employed two chief workers – Chen Gui, who was in charge of construction; and Wu Zhong, who was in charge of planning. It is commonly believed that a million workers were forced by the emperor's guards to build the City. Other tradesmen of slightly lesser importance were Lu Xiang (mason), Yang Qing (tiler) and Cai Xin (project manager). Although they might have been named for their involvement, architects and craftspeople did not receive much recognition for their work. They were considered to be merely servants of the emperor.

Materials – such as tiles, wood and marble – were sourced from across China, and shipped to Beijing using the network of canals that were built in the 6th and 7th centuries. Stone came from Fangshang county; marble and square paving tiles came from Xuzhou; wood came from Sichuan,

Guangdong and Yunnan; coloured stones came from Jixian county; granite from Quyang county; and roof tiles came from western Beijing. Bricks were sourced from Linqing and were made from a mixture of white lime and glutinous rice, while cement was

Emperor Yongle was the founder of the Ming dynasty (1368–1644). It was he who built the magnificent Forbidden City at the very heart of the new capital, Beijing.

A dynasty is a succession of rulers who share the same ancestor. A new dynasty could only come to power through overthrowing the previous dynasty. From the 3rd dynasty BC to the early 20th century, China had a total of 12 major dynastic periods. The first prehistoric dynasty is believed to be Xia, from about the 21st to the 16th century BC. The two dynasties that resided at the Forbidden City that stands today were the Ming (1368–1644) and Qing (1644–1912).

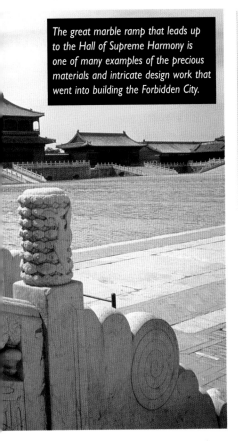

The great marble ramp that leads up to the Hall of Supreme Harmony is one of many examples of the precious materials and intricate design work that went into building the Forbidden City.

made from glutinous rice mixed with egg whites. Amazingly, this mixture made the bricks extremely strong, although light. Massive stones were also used in building parts of the City, such as the paths and courtyards. To move these from the canal to the city, workers dug a well every 50 metres along the road. In the winter, they poured water from the wells on to the road. When the water turned to ice, they could slide the stones along and into the city.

The Forbidden City was built within an enormous rectangle measuring 960 by 750 metres. The outer wall is 10 metres high and 8.6 metres wide at the base, narrowing at the top to prevent anyone from climbing it. There are only four gateways in this wall and a 52-metre wide moat around it. Inside are about 800 buildings with 9,999 rooms (– nine is a lucky number for the Chinese).

PLANNING AND CONSTRUCTION

Like all Chinese monuments, the Forbidden City is built to benefit from good 'yin' and 'yang' effects – in accordance with Feng Shui. Feng Shui is an important element of Chinese spiritual belief, which centres around what it considers to be the opposite forces in nature. 'Yin' is feminine and cool while 'yang' is masculine and hot.

During the Ming and Qing periods, Feng Shui was a secret, known only to a handful of astronomers and scientists charged with maintaining the health, wealth and power of the court.

The Chinese were not interested in building enduring monuments or impressive palaces like those built for European royalty. Instead, architecture was meant to reflect the balance of yin and yang and incorporate architects' and astronomers' specialist knowledge about designing buildings. So, before all the splendours of

The roofs and eaves of the palace buildings have been designed with great detail, many featuring carvings of animals.

decoration and ornament was added, architects had to plan where to position every building for the strongest spiritual benefit.

The Forbidden City faces south. It was laid out as a rectangle from north to south with the two main gates on the north and south wall and the buildings set out as a grid inside. Each building within the walls was positioned according to its function and status. All buildings were constructed on painted wooden platforms to protect them against damp. Also, giant bronze cauldrons filled with water were placed outside each building in case of fire. Chinese building procedures were the opposite of those used in most other countries. Instead of using walls and columns to hold up the roof, the Chinese first made the roof and then positioned columns beneath – usually, one in each corner was enough to hold up a roof, heavy with tiles. Walls were merely screens and not used for

Because most of the buildings at the City were made of wood, huge bronze cauldrons filled with water were placed outside each of the main buildings, in case fire broke out.

Tales & customs – PAPER WINDOWS

Paper was invented in China in the 2nd century BC. The earliest paper was made with plants such as hemp, but about a century later, rice, bamboo and wood were used. Many windows of the Forbidden City were called screens and were filled with rice paper instead of glass. In the winter, the paper kept out cold air and in the summer, it was pierced to let a gentle breeze into the rooms. The paper was often replaced. Paper windows were commonly used across China because they were more economical than glass.

support. Roof tiles were thick and semi-circular, unlike Western tiles, which are usually flat.

COLOUR AND SYMBOLISM

Symbols, usually representing long life, health, wealth and power, were used throughout the Forbidden City. Colours are particularly significant for the Chinese people. The main colours of the city are the crimson of the walls, representing joy, dignity and solemnity; and the yellow glazed tiles, representing glory, life and nourishment. Green represents harmony; white means purity and death; grey symbolises disaster; and black represents water. Platforms were painted white; pillars and walls red; and

The colours of the roofs at the Forbidden City traditionally represented the status or rank of the person who lived within.

the roofs of all imperial buildings were yellow (the colour reserved for the emperor); while temples had blue roofs. Purple often symbolises joy, happiness and heaven. Although the City was initially known as the 'Purple Forbidden City', there is not a lot of purple paintwork to be seen. This title is actually a metaphoric connection linking the home of the Emperor of Heaven to the symbolic colour of the North Star – believed at the time to be the centre of the Cosmos.

Animal statues guard many buildings at the Forbidden City. The male lion always has his right paw over a pomegranate, which was a symbol of power. Bronze turtles symbolise peace, and represent the emperor himself.

The colours used on the external façades of the Forbidden City buildings almost always had a purpose or symbolic meaning. For instance, on this building, red symbolises happiness whilst yellow (or gold) represents glory.

CHAPTER 2

The Forbidden City through history

During its time as a royal residence, 14 emperors of the Ming dynasty and ten emperors of the Qing dynasty reigned in the Forbidden City. It was built for privilege and power and yet became both a palace and a prison for those who lived there. Both the Ming and the Qing believed that their dynasties would last forever, yet five centuries after it was built; the last emperor left the Forbidden City, only to come back and work in the grounds as a gardener.

HOW THE CITY BEGAN

In 1211, the fierce and mighty warrior Genghis Khan took over China and set up the Mongol dynasty. Genghis Khan's grandson, Kublai Khan, later set up a new Mongol dynasty called the Yuan dynasty and built the first Forbidden City which he called 'Danei' in Beijing in the 13th century. Mongol emperors ruled China for over a century until, in the mid-14th century, there was a series of floods, poor harvests, poverty, disease and famine. By 1325, one of the famines had killed nearly eight million people. The peasants believed that the Mongols should have governed the country better and made sure that there was

The grandson of Genghis Khan, Kublai Khan established the Yuan dynasty which ruled until he was driven out by a rebellion from the people.

enough food for all. This caused several peasant revolts to break out across China in the 1350s.

A peasant named Zhu Yuanzhang then organised an army and conquered several regions across China. In 1368, he arrived in Beijing, expecting to face a Mongol army, but the Mongols had heard about him already and fled. So he started a new dynasty, which he called Ming and he ordered the destruction of the Mongol Yuan dynasty's Forbidden City, settling with his new court in Nanjing in the south. Calling himself Emperor Hongwu, Zhu Yuanzhang reigned until 1398 when his son Jianwen became the second Ming emperor. In 1402, Jianwen's uncle, Zhu Di, took the throne from Jianwen, becoming the third Ming emperor and naming himself Yongle.

Time line

1279	Mongols conquer China. Yuan dynasty established.
1368	The Ming dynasty is founded by Chu Yuanchang, under whose leadership China regains independence from the Mongols.
1368	The renovation of the Great Wall of China begins.
1405	The pirate Zheng He sails west with a fleet of 300 ships, invading Sumatra and Ceylon (now Sri Lanka) and reaching the coast of Africa.
1421	Construction of the Forbidden City begins in Beijing.
1500	Approximately 155 million people live under the Ming empire.

CHINESE CONTROL

Because the Ming emperors were Chinese, they felt more entitlement to reign over China than their predecessors. They quickly established a Chinese military to defend their land against outsiders. The Ming emperors reigned for 276 years, including 224 years within the Forbidden City.

Hongwu was a great leader and one of only three peasants ever to become emperor in China. He kept the land tax low and the granaries stocked to guard against famine. However, he believed that agriculture should be the country's only source of wealth and that trading with others was dishonourable. Hongwu admired

This 15th century silk painting features two members of court during the Ming dynasty.

military prowess and he developed a strong military to defend against any enemies. He also took control of nearly all aspects of government so that no other group could gain enough power to overthrow him.

Later, in the fourth year of his reign, Yongle decided to move his court back to the safer position of Beijing and had the Forbidden City rebuilt to protect himself and his court from enemies. He spent a huge amount of money rebuilding the Forbidden City, moving it slightly to the south of the former Mongol capital, so that it would be in the exact centre of Beijing. Once it was built, no other country in the world had a palace of such size, complexity and grandeur, but then, no other country was as big. About 120

This vase painting shows gardeners watering tea plants. Tea was not a source of trade for China until the 17th century.

1550   The renovation of the Great Wall of China is completed.

1557   Portugal establishes a trading post in Macao (first European settlement in the Far East).

1616   Nurhachi unifies the Manchus and creates the state of Qing (Jin) in northeastern China.

1637   The Manchus, led by Nurhachi's son Abahai, invade Korea and Korea becomes a vassal state of the Manchus.

This silk painting from 1500 shows a priest standing in front of the Forbidden City.

One of the Great Wonders of the World, the Great Wall of China was built more than 2,000 years ago to act as a defence against attackers. It stretches 2,400 kilometres (1,500 miles) from east to west China.

million people – more than the entire population of Europe – lived in China and the emperor ruled over them all.

For more than 500 years, emperors of two dynasties lived in luxury and seclusion, carrying out the affairs of state from the Forbidden City. Over that time, Yongle's original planning and ideas were hardly altered. The palace reflected power, wealth and superiority. The Ming also poured money and manpower into rebuilding and extending the Great Wall of China, which was another way that the emperors

protected themselves from outside attackers. Although this autocratic way of life may have seemed like a good idea at the time, it had many flaws. Most people living in the Forbidden City, particularly the emperors and empresses themselves, became out of touch with the rest of China. They followed elaborate daily rituals that had little to do with the outside world. Inefficiency and corruption followed, and the ordinary people who lived in poverty outside the City often rose up and rebelled. Some emperors gave their servants or wives more responsibility, which meant that many people used their positions of power for personal advantage and not for the good of the people. A small number of people held too much power, although at the time it seemed to the Chinese that this was the only way to live.

MONEY, BOOKS AND ART

From the beginning of the Ming dynasty, money was a problem. Paper notes and coins were considered to only represent real money that was kept in the

country's treasury, usually in gold bars. When a country made more notes or coins than it had in gold, people began to lose faith in the money and it became devalued. At the beginning of the Ming dynasty, paper money (which the Chinese invented in the 10th century) was used. But Hongwu printed more paper money than he had gold in his treasury, so by 1425, 27 years after his death and five years after the Forbidden City

was built, Chinese currency was worth 1/70th of its original value. So, paper money was abandoned and copper coins were used once more. However, the government did not make enough of these and people began counterfeiting, which caused the coins to be worth even less. Despite this, there were great intellectual innovations in China under the Ming. One development of the dynasty was the fictional novel.

Because these novels developed from Chinese storytellers, they were written in everyday words rather than the exclusive language of the nobility, which most Chinese people could not understand. Chapters ended at points where storytellers would have stopped to collect money from listeners, which is why they are gripping – you would have to pay to find out what happened next! The first encyclopedias and

dictionaries were also produced during this time. In 1615, a dictionary that reduced the number of 'radicals' was published. Radicals are the signs which

Hand-dyeing silk was one of the many specialist crafts that flourished under the Ming dynasty.

1729	Emperor Yongzheng is told about the growing use of opium, but takes no action.
1801	China's population is 295 million.
1830	Corruption, decentralisation of power, popular rebellions.
1839	A Chinese attempt at suppressing the illicit British trade in opium causes the Opium war.

The Forbidden City

This banknote from the Ming Dynasty was worth 1000 cash coins in 1374. Later, the value of currency dropped dramatically.

– became popular during the Ming dynasty. Craftsmen produced colourful wood-block prints that depicted interesting and amusing stories, while other craftsmen created the delicately patterned blue-and-white porcelain vases and jars in the Ming style that is valuable today. Some Ming porcelain was decorated in three colours, but the most well-known was just blue and white. Although trade was initially frowned upon, by the mid-15th century, China had established sea routes that were used for trade with Japan and south Asia, and was far ahead of the rest of the world in naval capabilities. During the Ming dynasty, naval expeditions were extended and some Europeans were permitted at court.

DOWNFALL OF THE MING DYNASTY

Emperor Yongle aimed to restore China to the dominant position it had held in Asia at the beginning of the 14th century.

combine to make up the hundreds of characters in the Chinese written language. This simplification of the language made it much easier for people to learn to read and write.

Education was valued highly and educated Chinese people became interested in philosophy, religion and art. Two crafts invented by the Chinese – wood-block printing and porcelain production

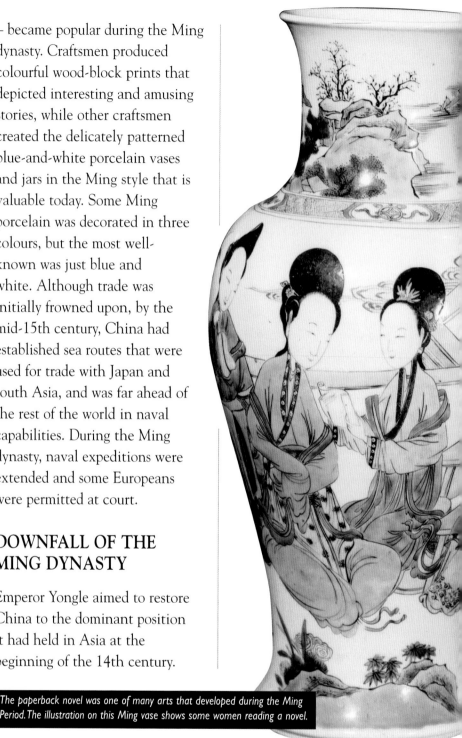

The paperback novel was one of many arts that developed during the Ming Period. The illustration on this Ming vase shows some women reading a novel.

Time line

1842	Under the Treaty of Nanjing, China cedes the island of Hong Kong to Britain.
1851	The Taiping rebels, led by a village teacher, Hong Xiuquan, stage an anti-Manchu rebellion that will last 14 years (30 million people killed).
1860	Russia secures north Manchuria.
1884	France expands in Indochina after winning a war against China.
1895	China is forced to cede Taiwan and recognise Japanese sovereignty over Korea.

He intended for the new Forbidden City to represent the almighty power of the Ming dynasty, believing that this would be the best way to rule China. But it had many faults, and although its power was great, the dynasty eventually fell. Most emperors who lived within the city walls were distant from their subjects, both mentally and physically, and did not know what the people really needed. Some emperors came to power as children and were overshadowed by their employees who gained a lot of the power for themselves. For example, Emperor Wanli (1573–1620), tired of the burdens of power, handed most of his responsibilities to his courtiers. This did not please the people who were further angered when taxes were raised to support the extravagant lifestyle of the court. As had occurred during previous dynasties, rebellions broke out outside the Forbidden City as people became discontented. Meanwhile, the Manchu became angry that some cities in their own country, Manchuria (to the northeast of China), were populated entirely by Chinese people. So the Manchu attacked these cities and forced the Chinese out, eventually gaining control of the whole of Manchuria. They didn't let it stop there, however, and proceeded to march on into China. In 1644, a rebel named Li Zicheng gathered an army, entered Beijing and seized power. On learning that Li Zicheng had seized Beijing, Emperor Chongzhen hanged himself in a park behind the Forbidden City. He was the last Ming emperor.

The distinctive blue-and-white patterns denote the main Ming porcelain style.

THE QING DYNASTY

The first Qing emperor, Shunzhi, was Manchurian. He started the dynasty by exterminating all the other rebels except those from Manchu. Therefore, emperors of the Qing (pronounced 'ching') dynasty were foreign like the Yuan dynasty, making them the second foreign dynasty to rule China. The Qing ruled for 268 years, from 1644 to 1911 and the reigns of three of its first emperors were peaceful and prosperous. These three rulers provided strong leadership for 133 years. They were Kangxi (reigned 1662–1722); Yongzheng (reigned 1722–1736) and Qianlong (reigned 1736–1796). They retained many of the attitudes, ideas and rules of the Ming and encouraged Chinese officials to serve them. They

1898	The 'Hundred Days' Reform' fails when the mother of the emperor, Tsu Hsi, has him arrested and confined in the Forbidden City.
1900	The anti-western Boxer (Yihetuan) rebellion is crushed by foreign troops (Russia, Britain, France, Japan, USA) and Tsu Hsi flees to the mountains. China's population is 467 million.
1911	Riots cause the collapse of the Qing dynasty and Republican China is born, but power is seized by Yuan Shikai and 11 million die.

The Forbidden City

Despite the fact that the Manchu were renowned for their military power, their Qing Dynasty was a relatively peaceful one.

continued to modernise farming, started under the Ming dynasty, and organised their government in an extremely efficient way. During the period, taxes were generally light and international trade grew. Books, printing, painting and porcelain production improved even more, leading to a revival of arts and learning. But Qing emperors and courts were set in their ways and things did not change much in the following centuries. When the West wanted to trade with them for valuable Chinese goods, Qing emperors feared that wealthy European merchants would undermine their authority. The Qing restricted trade heavily, and so prevented the Chinese economy from growing as fast as it might have done. Later, wars with western powers, including Britain, France and Japan, left the Qing weakened and eventually, internal rebellions left them unable to cope with the needs of such a vast country. Beyond the walls, great cultural, social, technological and political changes occurred over the centuries; but within the walls, life remained inflexible and disciplined.

NO LONGER FORBIDDEN

From the 19th century, as a result of war, a number of Chinese cities were taken over by some more powerful western countries. China was being weakened, but inside the Forbidden City, no-one knew. Eventually, on October 10, 1911, a revolution transformed China from an imperial empire into a republic and outside the Forbidden City, the Nationalist Party took control. In 1912, the last Qing emperor, Puyi, abdicated because the Prime Minister had

This painting shows the representatives of many countries attending a ceremony to honour Emperor Qianlong of the Qing dynasty.

taken control of China, calling it a new Republic. Puyi kept the title of emperor and the royal family were allowed to stay in the Forbidden City. There he remained until 1924, when he was forced to sign documents saying that he was just an ordinary Chinese citizen and made to leave the Forbidden City. From 1927, there was conflict between the

Time line		
1924	Puyi, the last emperor, leaves the Forbidden City.	
1931	Japan invades Manchuria. Great floods in China.	
1934	Mao Zedong leads the 'Long March' of the communist Red Army (170,000 die).	
1937	Japan invades China and captures Nanjing.	
1945	World War II ends and Japan is forced to retreat.	
1945	At the end of World War II the Korean peninsula is occupied by the Soviet Union (north) and the USA (south).	
1948	Communist North Korea declares independence.	
1949	Mao Zedong proclaims the People's Republic of China.	
1950	Communist North Korea, helped by China, attacks capitalist South Korea, but the invasion fails after USA intervention.	

fighting between the Nationalist Party and the Communist Party turned into civil war. After nearly three years of war, the Communists won and Mao Zedong stood at the Gate of Heavenly Peace in front of the Forbidden City to announce the founding of the People's Republic of China. The new Communist government aimed to create a new, fair society for all, completely different to the previous system that had allowed one man to have total power. Mao Zedong's Red Guards tried to destroy traditional customs, books and clothes. People who spoke out of turn were either killed or sent to work in labour camps. Thousands of people were exiled and trade with the West was stopped. It seemed that in getting rid of the emperors, China had simply replaced them with another strict regime. The ten years before Chairman Mao's death in 1976 were known as the 'Ten Years of Chaos'.

Communists and the Nationalists. By the end of 1934, 'the Red Army' (about 100,000 people who believed in Communism), left Jiangxi to travel to Yan'an. They marched through many provinces, climbed over 18 mountain ranges, crossed 24 rivers and trekked through marshes and deserts, led by Mao Zedong, a former teacher. Only one in every five people who set out on the march survived. They made Yan'an their headquarters until 1946, when

The last emperor to reside at the Forbidden City was the Qing emperor, Puyi. In 1912, Puyi abdicated the throne and China became a republic.

1950 Mao orders the persecution of landlords, causing the deaths of about one million people.
1958 Mao's 'Great Leap Forward' causes between 16 and 30 million people to die due to famine.
1966 Mao launches the 'Cultural Revolution'. Millions die in the next three years.
1972 US President Richard Nixon formally recognises Communist China as a country.
1981 The Communist Party formally condemns Mao for the economic disasters from 1957 until his death.

CHAPTER 3

Explore the Forbidden City

The Forbidden City is deep in the centre of Beijing. It is divided into three main areas. The first part at the south end is the great courtyard, between the Meridian Gate and the Gate of Supreme Harmony. This was where people waited if they wanted to catch a glimpse of the emperor. The second area is the Outer Court, containing three palaces where business and ceremony took place. The third area, at the north end of the city, is the Inner Court – the tightly guarded area where the emperor lived with his family.

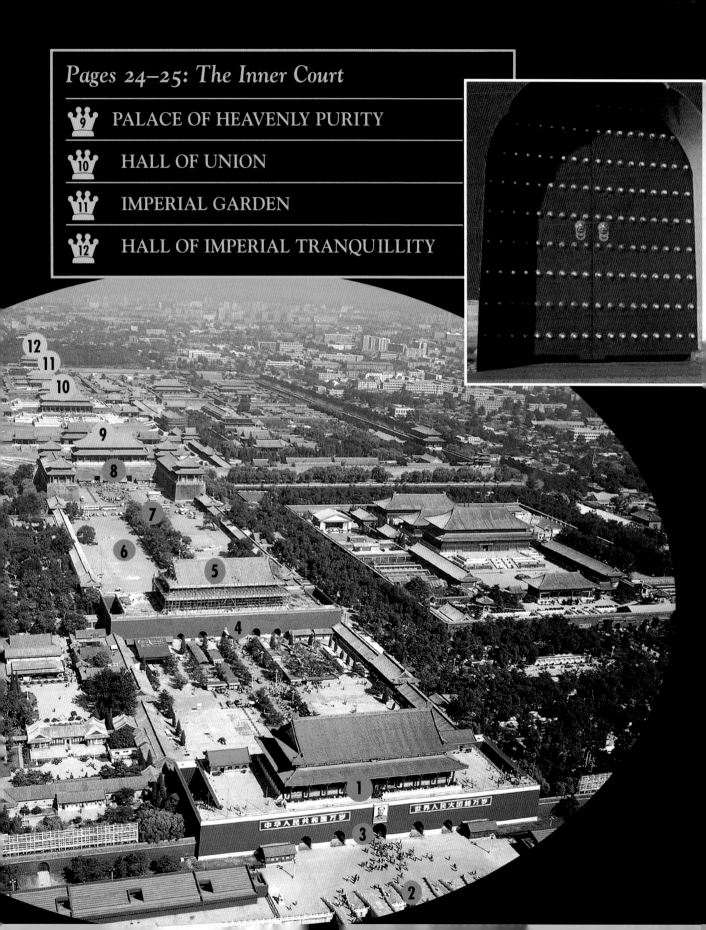

The Forbidden City

中华人民共和国万岁

 ## GATE OF HEAVENLY PEACE

Originally, there were eight gates that had to be passed through before reaching the Great Courtyard. Not all of the gates are still there, but one gate in particular leads up to the beginning of the Great Courtyard. This is the **GATE OF HEAVENLY PEACE**, or Tiananmen. Tiananmen Gate was originally built during the Ming dynasty, and rebuilt in 1651. It marks the passage from the Imperial City to the Forbidden City. There are balconies over the gate, from where the emperor would announce important messages or send off his generals with great ceremony if they were going to war. Even now, the Chinese army still raises the national flag from here, every day at dawn. The square to the south of Tiananmen was the site of the most shocking event in recent Chinese history, the massacre of over 2,000 pro-democracy protesters in June, 1989.

The tallest building of the Forbidden City is its main entrance. The Meridian Gate is 80 metres tall and an imposing structure. The emperor used to survey his troops from the great pavilion above the central gate.

2 MERIDIAN GATE

The **MERIDIAN GATE** stands at the southern entrance to the Forbidden City. This gate, which was built in 1417, stands imposingly in the massive outer wall and leads directly into the Great Courtyard. At 40 metres long, the Meridian Gate is the tallest building of the Forbidden City. Chinese emperors believed that the gateway lay on a significant line in the centre of the world and directly beneath the Sun. The grand gate has five openings and is topped by five pavilions, named Five Phoenix Tower. There were strict rules to follow when people entered the Forbidden City. The emperor was the only person allowed through the central gateway, except for the empress on her wedding day.

The Gate of Heavenly Peace is illuminated in the evening. A portrait of Mao Zedong hangs on the outside along with the words: 'Long Live the People's Republic of China'.

👑3 INNER GOLDEN RIVER

The moat around the Forbidden City was called the Outer Golden Water River or Golden River. The Meridian Gate opens on to a courtyard that is 200 metres long and 130 metres wide. Here, the Golden River continues to flow but as a smaller river, which when inside the City, is called the **INNER GOLDEN RIVER**. Five gleaming white marble bridges span the Inner Golden River. The bridges were decorated with marble balustrades carved with dragons and a phoenix. The river was close at hand in case of fire, as well as for decoration.

The Outer Golden River flows in an arc shape and can be crossed by any one of five marble bridges.

👑4 GATE OF SUPREME HARMONY

On the other side of this courtyard is the **GATE OF SUPREME HARMONY**. This gate rises up across the Inner Golden River, blocking off the next and largest courtyard, the Outer Court. The Gate of Supreme Harmony is the tallest gatehouse in the Forbidden City. Two large bronze lions guard the stairs to the gatehouse. These are classic Chinese symbols of power and dignity – guardians of the rich and the powerful. The lion on the right is the male, with a ball under his foot, meaning that imperial power extended worldwide. The lioness on the west puts her front left paw on a lion cub, indicating a prosperous, growing family.

The double-roofed Gate of Supreme Harmony stands on a terrace before a large, open marble square.

 ## HALL OF SUPREME HARMONY

Through the Gate of Supreme Harmony is the Outer Court, which contains three Halls of Harmony. The first, the **HALL OF SUPREME HARMONY**, is the largest hall in the Forbidden City. This is the most important building in the City, first built in about 1418 and restored in the 17th century. Great ceremonies, banquets, coronations and meetings were held here. The large bronze turtle at the entrance has a removable lid. On special occasions, incense was lit inside so that smoke billowed from the mouth. Inside, the hall is decorated in red and gold, with 24 marble columns beneath a double-curved roof and a richly decorated dragon throne – where the emperor sat. Around the throne stand two bronze cranes, an elephant-shaped incense burner and tripods in the shape of mythical beasts.

The grand Throne Platform resides inside the Hall of Supreme Harmony in the Outer Court of the Forbidden City.

 ## OUTER COURT

The massive **OUTER COURT** is more than 30,000 square metres in area and its three halls are vast and imposing palaces, built for important functions in the daily life of the emperor. There are no trees on the square as the emperors were believed to be Sons of Heaven, and therefore, occupy the highest position in the country. An 'imperial road' crosses the court. This is a pathway picked out in stone across the brick-paved courtyard. At ceremonies, guards would be stationed on the great terrace of the Outer Court, carrying between them more than 200 ceremonial objects of silver and gold. Two orchestras would play and perfume would rise from bronze urns that were filled with either burning pine branches or scented oil floating on water.

The Outer Court was the open space within the City where more of the public imperial business and festivities took place.

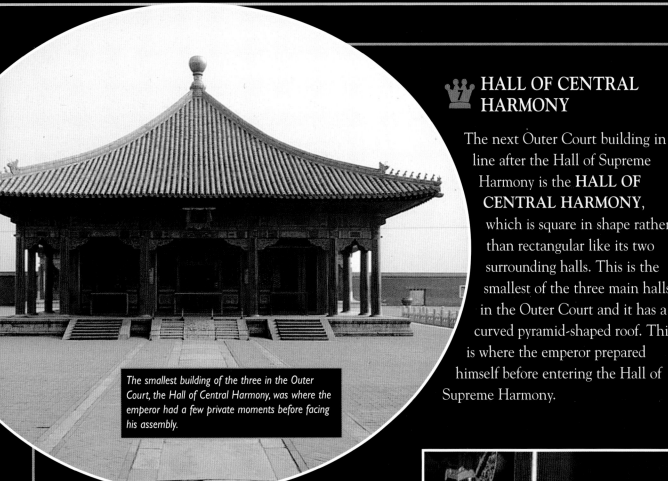

The smallest building of the three in the Outer Court, the Hall of Central Harmony, was where the emperor had a few private moments before facing his assembly.

♕ HALL OF CENTRAL HARMONY

The next Outer Court building in line after the Hall of Supreme Harmony is the **HALL OF CENTRAL HARMONY**, which is square in shape rather than rectangular like its two surrounding halls. This is the smallest of the three main halls in the Outer Court and it has a curved pyramid-shaped roof. This is where the emperor prepared himself before entering the Hall of Supreme Harmony.

♕ HALL OF PRESERVING HARMONY

The third hall in this court is the **HALL OF PRESERVING HARMONY** which is built in the same style as the Hall of Supreme Harmony, although smaller. Apart from the empress on her wedding day, no women were admitted to the three halls in the Outer Court. Three doorways on the north side of this hall open on to steps and a carved marble ramp which leads to the Gate of Heavenly Purity – which separated the official Outer Court from the private Inner Court.

The massive red columns that support the exterior of the Hall of Preserving Harmony mirror those of the Hall's interior.

9 PALACE OF HEAVENLY PURITY

The Inner Court was one of the most private parts of the Forbidden City. It was where the emperor and his family lived. The first and most important building here is the **PALACE OF HEAVENLY PURITY**, which housed the throne room and imperial bedchamber. It was also used as offices for later emperors. Banquets were held here for New Year and other festivals and emperors' coffins waited here before their funerals. The throne is magnificent – gold, decorated with glittering rubies and emeralds. Behind the throne is a gilded screen, covered with quotations from ancient Chinese philosophy and written in beautiful calligraphy.

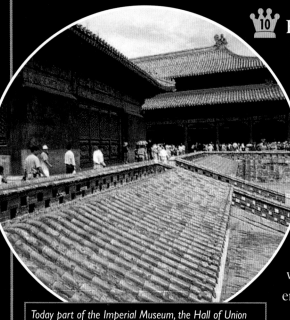

10 HALL OF UNION

The second of these Inner Court palaces is built on a square like the Hall of Central Harmony and was called the **HALL OF UNION**. With its water clock, golden ceiling and golden ball suspended from the centre, this was the empresses' throne room. Leading on from the Hall of Union, is the Palace of Earthly Tranquillity where Ming empresses lived. It was also used as a special wedding chamber and a shrine where some emperors worshipped.

Today part of the Imperial Museum, the Hall of Union houses the imperial seals – the emperor's signature stamps. Each is made of gold, jade and sandalwood.

The Palace of Heavenly Purity was one of the original Ming buildings built in 1420 for the emperor to live in.

IMPERIAL GARDEN

The carefully cultivated plants and rocks in the Imperial Garden were designed to inspire peace.

To the north, through the Gate of Earthly Tranquillity is the **IMPERIAL GARDEN**, spreading over 12,000 square metres. It was designed to be a space for relaxation and contemplation. This is where emperors came to rest. Garden planning in China was counted as an extension of architectural planning and design. The landscaped gardens contained purposefully placed rocks, trees, rockeries, walkways and pavilions. Emperor Qianlong wrote of the garden: 'Every ruler, when he has returned from audience and has finished his public duties, must have a garden in which he may stroll, look around and relax his heart.'

HALL OF IMPERIAL TRANQUILLITY

In the centre of the garden, is the **HALL OF IMPERIAL TRANQUILLITY** (or Peace), the best preserved of all the Ming buildings. Inside is a statue of Xuan Wu, the water god, who required lots of encouragement in the form of daily offerings to protect the whole of the Forbidden City from fire. Nearby, there are many other buildings surrounding the three courts, such as living quarters for the emperor's family and servants, libraries, theatres, kitchens and storage halls. A distinctive building within view is the Temple of Heaven – a circular building situated on a three-layered platform.

From the Hall of Imperial Tranquillity, many surrounding buildings can be seen, such as the circular Temple of Heaven.

CHAPTER 4

The People

At the end of the 18th century, about 9,000 people lived in the Forbidden City. Chinese people believed that the emperor was the 'Son of Heaven' and the link between the people and God. No-one questioned how emperors lived – they had complete power and could do as they pleased. This power protected emperors, but also isolated them. Although many emperors improved life for their subjects, most had no idea about the hardships many people suffered outside the Forbidden City.

THE EMPERORS

Under the Ming emperors, the population of China doubled. Educated Chinese people learned about philosophy, religion and art. Yongle and emperors after him

Under the Ming dynasty, educated people became learned and mastered the arts. This Ming silk painting depicts a household scene.

expanded sea trade and expeditions as well as trade and industry. They also encouraged eminent Europeans to enter the Forbidden City and meet with important Chinese officials. But for all this forward thinking, the Ming dynasty became weak when emperors became too isolated and were not aware of the poverty of some of their subjects, or gave too much power to their immediate servants. When the Qing dynasty came to power, they had other ideas. They tried a new method of government, giving power to officials other than those only in the Inner Court. Emperor Kangxi, the longest ruling emperor, secured the borders of China, improved agriculture, built-up the textile industry and also encouraged the arts and crafts and book publishing. Some of this helped peasants all over China,

giving them valuable work. Kangxi's successors, Yongzheng, his 11th son and Qianlong, his grandson, continued to strengthen the country. All emperors spent most of their days attending official duties; the daily running of the place was ruled by codes of behaviour (protocol) and rituals. To relax, they walked in the Imperial Garden, prayed or meditated, played chess, wrote poetry and calligraphy, or played the qin, a seven-stringed instrument. Some also raised grasshoppers for amusement!

Eating was a big part of the day. Unless they were at a banquet, emperors ate alone. They were served breakfast at dawn, dinner at midday and supper at sunset. Generally there were eight main dishes, four side dishes, two or three hot soups, hotpots and steamed buns, rice, cakes and herbal teas to drink. Any food that was left over was sent to their wives and concubines and any remaining food after that, was given to the servants. Court life was organised around tradition and formal procedures and courtiers had to follow set codes of dress and behaviour. Ministers and officials had to prostrate themselves nine times when they appeared before the emperor, which meant bowing, kneeling and touching the ground with their foreheads nine times.

QIANLONG

Qianlong was sophisticated and learned. He admired and enjoyed all the arts and regularly visited the palace workshops to see artefacts being made. From the age of six he worked hard

Emperor Qianlong (1711–99) was the fourth emperor of the Manchu or Qing dynasty.

Tales & customs – SPECIAL EVENTS

A number of special events took place at the Meridian Gate (the southern entrance to the Forbidden City). On the equivalent of October 1, the emperor would make public the solar calendar for the coming year. The calendar indicated the days on which the various annual ceremonies would be held. In ancient times, emperors gave food to ministers at the Gate to mark important days in the year. Following a war, the emperor would personally receive captives here also.

The Forbidden City

The specialist art of calligraphy prospered under Qianlong's leadership.

everyday at calligraphy, writing poetry, painting and reading the classics and philosophy. He had several learned advisors around him in the Forbidden Palace, such as an Italian priest, who was also a painter and architect, and a French mathematician and astronomer. He commissioned many books and works of art and collected many ornaments and artworks, such as paintings, carved jade and pieces of calligraphy, keeping a detailed catalogue of everything. During his reign, the arts – such as painting, calligraphy and enamel and inlay work – really flourished. Qianlong's working days usually began at about 3 am and continued to about 10 pm. From within the city, he discussed problems of the country with his ministers, planning solutions, and initiated military expeditions. However, his reign was not perfect and he gave

Tales & customs – CLEVER BEASTS

In one of the great halls of the Forbidden City, the Hall of Central Harmony, there are two golden unicorns, one on each side of the throne. These were called 'luduan' in Chinese and were believed to be capable of travelling 9,000 kilometres a day and speaking many languages. Since these divine beasts could see and tell so much, they were put beside the throne to indicate the wisdom and foresight of the emperors. Also on either side of the throne are two sedan chairs that were used to transport emperors around the Forbidden City.

too much power to some of his favourites. Power made many greedy and if the favouritism ended, the penalty was often severe. For instance, Qianlong gave a huge amount of power to a Manchu general named Heshen. Heshen spent a lot of money and was seen to have too much influence over Qianlong. So when Qianlong died, Heshen was ordered to commit suicide.

power), Christianity, Confucianism and Islam; although China's primary religion was Buddhism. After 60 years of rule he retired, out of respect for his grandfather Kangxi, who had reigned for 61 years.

THE SUCCESSION

Who would be the next emperor had become a bit of a problem, as

The Emperor Qianlong formally receives a party of visitors at the Forbidden City.

These pottery figurines from the Qianlong period depict female attendants bearing food.

Emperors had several wives and female companions. (Emperors were allowed these female companions, who were like unofficial wives and known as concubines.) For example, Qianlong had two official wives, 29 concubines and 26 children. Qianlong was also a great military man. A tolerant ruler, he allowed several religions to be practised during his reign, including Daoism (although he limited the Daoists'

emperors usually had several sons by different wives and concubines. So, a system developed, where the emperor's choice of successor was kept secret until after their death. The emperor would have written the name of his choice of successor on a document and kept it concealed within his robes. He would also have written the same name on another document and put it into a sealed box. On the emperor's death, both documents would be taken and compared. One name would be on both documents and that person was the new emperor.

THE LAST EMPEROR

The 'last emperor', Puyi, succeeded to the throne at the age of three in 1908. He was forced to abdicate in 1912, but stayed in the Forbidden City until 1924, learning to read and write and practising calligraphy for hours every day. During this time, he learned to ride a bicycle and play tennis. He remained a symbol of importance for many people.

WOMEN OF THE COURT

Twelve palaces, divided into six on each side of the Inner Court, were homes for the wives, concubines and other female relatives of the emperor. Behind these two groups

of palaces were the green-roofed buildings reserved for the infant princes. The only woman who did not live in any part of these palaces was the emperor's mother, the highest ranking woman in the country, known as the dowager empress. She lived in The Palace of Benevolent Tranquillity, a great big complex of palaces to the east of the Gate of Heavenly Purity.

Empresses, other wives and concubines were always of high birth before they entered the Forbidden City. Once married, the emperor gave each of his wives an important rank, although he always had a 'number one wife' who was the empress and the second most important woman in the city. Although the dowager empress was more

Women of the court were governed by strict protocol. The ivory sculpture above depicts Kuan Yin, a goddess from the Qian period – she was believed to possess all the ideal womanly virtues, such as compassion, mercy and modesty.

Tales & customs – EVERY DETAIL COUNTS

No detail was spared in ensuring the Forbidden City was perfectly built. Even the ground was laid in a particular way – seven layers length-wise and eight layers cross-wise, each on top of the other, totalling 15 layers. The purpose of this was to protect the City against assassins digging tunnels into the palace. Even the bricks were specially made to sound nice when walked upon. The rooms on each side were said to serve as warehouses for storing such items as fur, porcelain, silver, tea, silk, satin and clothes.

Emperors were entitled to have more than one wife at a time. This 19th century painting shows a wedding ceremony taking place during the Qing Dynasty.

important, the empress was the person who governed the affairs of the Inner Court. Depending on their positions, wives had to follow rules, such as wearing a certain number of pearls on their hats; the colour and quality of their ceremonial clothes or the amount and type of food they were served. Different ranking wives ate from different coloured crockery. Only the emperor and empress were entitled to use real gold or 'radiant yellow' porcelain. All Qing wives and concubines were Manchu – no Chinese women were permitted. Imperial women made silk, prepared cakes and looked after the children. On the death of the emperor, wives and concubines retired to a vast complex of palaces to the west of the Inner Court.

Ming women had their feet bound as children so that they grew up with small feet – which was seen as the height of attractiveness at the time. Qing women were forbidden to do this as foot-binding was considered too 'Ming' for them. Instead, they wore shoes with extremely high porcelain platforms.

DRAGON LADY

In 1861, when her husband, Emperor Xianfeng died at the age of 30, Empress Cixi refused to retire to one of the outer palaces as tradition demanded. Instead, she ruled as Regent for her son (Xianfeng's only son), who was five years old and only lived until his teens.

The Empress Dowager Cixi (1835–1908) ruled as Regent for her son after her husband died.

The Forbidden City

When he died, she placed her four-year-old nephew on the throne. He only lived until his mid-30s. So in effect, she ruled over China for 48 years, sitting on her throne each morning to receive visitors and eventually dying in 1908 when two-year-old Puyi came to the throne. Empress Cixi rebuilt many of the palaces in the Forbidden City, restoring, repairing and improving many of the original buildings that had been built by Yongle. In 1885, in the year of her 50th birthday, she had the Palace of Concentrated Beauty completely refurbished. She had a little theatre built in one area of the palace and in the courtyard, bronze dragons and deer – good luck symbols – were added. Cixi lived in this palace for ten years with 180 servants, before moving on to the Palace of Peaceful Longevity. Empress Dowager Cixi has gone down in history as the Dragon Lady because of her ruthlessness, drive and cunning.

Many eunuchs resided at the Forbidden City. This photograph of a eunuch of the last dynasty was taken by Henri Cartier Bresson in 1949.

OTHER PEOPLE IN THE FORBIDDEN CITY

While women and children in the emperor's family lived in the palace, adult males generally did not. The only men allowed in the living areas of the palace at night were servants called eunuchs. Chinese eunuchs were men who had their penis and testicles surgically removed. Usually taking place before puberty, the operation meant that

the male body would not produce testosterone – so the man would never develop certain male characteristics, such as growing facial hair and gaining a deep voice. A eunuch could also never produce children. Eunuchs were considered 'safe' and loyal members of the royal court. Some eunuchs becoming extremely powerful in running and organising the court, while others were treated like slaves. The number of eunuchs working in the Forbidden City varied

Tales & customs – UNUSUAL EUNUCHS

Ordinary Chinese men were not allowed inside the Forbidden City, which is why all male workers were emasculated by removal of their testicles and penis, making them eunuchs. Eunuchs tested everything on behalf of the emperor, including tasting his food and testing his urine to make sure he was healthy. Young princes were raised almost exclusively by eunuchs. There are several stories of corrupt and power-hungry eunuchs who were believed to have manipulated the attitudes of the young prince in their care to suit their own needs.

This painting features court ladies combing and spinning silk, during the Northern Song dynasty in the early 12th century. Silk weaving was one of many artistic enterprises prized at court.

time there, respected for their scientific knowledge and artistic skills. As well, priestess-magicians performed rituals in the city, to the sound of drums, they went into a trance, making predictions and performing exorcisms. Priests of other religions, in particular, Buddhism, were always present.

greatly according to the period. In the Ming court, it is said that there were about 20,000, but Kangxi reduced the number to 9,000 and Qianlong to 3,000. At the fall of the Qing Dynasty, there were no more than 1,500. You might wonder why anyone would become a eunuch, but for every one of them, it was their only hope of escaping poverty and they either volunteered or were sold by their parents. Sadly, only half of them survived the operation that made them eunuchs. Maids also worked in the Forbidden City. They entered at 13 and spent a year training for whichever particular skill they were to have. Then they worked for about three or four years and were sent out of the city to get married. Maids who left the Forbidden City were never

allowed to return. Some people were employed in the Forbidden City who lived outside. These included guards who protected the city, domestic servants who carried out the lowliest tasks, and gardeners. Scholars entered the Forbidden City to take exams. They were chosen by an entrance exam, which was very difficult. Those who passed sat another exam in the Forbidden City, which was even tougher, creating a tradition of pride and importance in academic achievement.

Throughout the history of the city, various people of different religions and races often passed through. For example, Jesuit missionaries from Europe spent

Many different religious figures were drawn to China, such as European Jesuit missionaries like the one pictured.

CHAPTER 5

Significant events

M any festivals were celebrated in the Forbidden City. The most important of these was the New Year. The old Chinese calendar was completely different from that used in the west, with its months following the Moon rather than the Sun. Because of this, every few years an extra month had to be added, so dates vary each year and the Chinese New Year falls at some time between the middle of January to early March.

CHINESE NEW YEAR

Traditionally, the New Year was a time to make a complete new start. All the rooms in the Forbidden City were cleaned. Everything, including pictures, statues and furniture, was thoroughly scrubbed. The empress oversaw this, having first chosen a lucky day on which to start the cleaning, as everything followed good omens or lucky signs. Then special guests were invited to the celebrations. Everyone had new clothes for the last day of the old year and even the royal elephants had new headwear. Special steamed, not baked, cakes were made to be placed before the Buddhas and other religious statues around the city. It was believed that the higher the cakes rose, the happier the gods became. As well, small plates of dates and fresh fruit decorated with evergreen plants were placed before images of

Buddha and glass dishes filled with sweets were offered to the 'god of the kitchen'. This god was important at that time, as the Chinese believed that on the 23rd day of the last Moon, the god of

People in dragon costume is one of many colourful sights to be seen during Chinese New Year celebrations.

the kitchen went to visit the King of Heaven, where he reported on all that everyone had been doing in the Forbidden City that year. The sweets were meant to stick

his mouth together, to prevent him from telling too much.

Just before New Year's Eve, all the emperor's guests and high-ranking members of the court received beautifully written letters from the emperor, wishing them luck, long life and prosperity. Gifts were exchanged, the most lavish given to the emperor and empress and then the emperor gave out small amounts of money to everyone – thought to be a lucky omen. Festivities followed, lasting all night.

FESTIVAL OF LANTERNS

The New Year celebrations ended on the 15th day of the first moon with the Festival of Lanterns. Brightly coloured gauze lanterns of dragons, animals, flowers and fruits were strung across the courtyards and everyone wore colourful costumes. There was music and dancing, and the

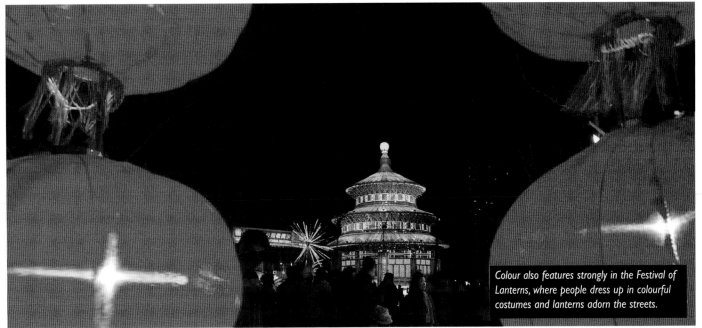

Colour also features strongly in the Festival of Lanterns, where people dress up in colourful costumes and lanterns adorn the streets.

evening ended with a grand firework display. The fireworks told stories about the history of China or lit up the sky as sparkling flowers and fruits. Portable wooden houses were made especially for the Imperial family and guests to watch while keeping out of the cold night air. But wooden houses and fireworks don't always mix and huge cauldrons of water were placed nearby in case of fire.

Fireworks are generally a big part of celebrations and festivals at the Forbidden City.

OTHER CEREMONIES

The Outer Court was the site for most other festivities, such as the accession of a new emperor to the throne, birthdays, weddings and the arrival of spring or autumn. These were all announced by drum rolls and music. In the courtyard before the Hall of Supreme Harmony, rows of court officials took up positions according to rank, guided by bronze markers set in the ground.

Tales & customs – WEDDINGS AND PARTIES

Emperors' weddings were extremely ornate. Most people were dressed in red and gold, and the bride had her head covered throughout the ceremony. There was a lot of dancing and music at all festivals — many dances told stories about the emperor's ancestors. Near the Imperial Garden, in the courtyard of the Study of Fresh Fragrance, Emperor Qianlong had a two-storey theatre and banqueting and concert hall built for the imperial family to celebrate the Spring Festival each year.

CHAPTER 6

Uncovering the past

A lot of the beautiful ornaments and furnishings were either taken from the Forbidden City or damaged. While many fires were accidental, some fires were started deliberately by eunuchs and other court officials who could get rich on repair bills. Sadly though, rare books, paintings and calligraphy were also lost.
In the last years of the empire, Emperor Puyi stole or pawned huge numbers of cultural relics. In the 20th century there were two major lootings of the city, and many of the valuable relics were taken away. Now many of these are in museums elsewhere.

RELICS RECOVERED

In the 1950s, after more than ten years of hard work, searching and questioning, by Chinese government officials, about 710,000 relics from the Forbidden City during the Qing dynasty were retrieved, some of them the same objects that Puyi had pawned to make money for himself! At the same time, through donations and even more rigorous searching, over 220,000 further objects were found and added to the collection. These included ancient paintings, ornaments, scrolls and intricate calligraphy. To keep these safe, from the 1950s onwards, the museum's storehouses were completely repaired to provide a damp- and insect-proof environment for the treasures. Then, in the 1990s an even newer storehouse with a capacity for over 600,000 items was built, with

This vase was made during the Qianlong period of the Qing dynasty and is part of the museum collection today.

controls for maintaining a constant temperature and humidity as well as defence against fire and theft. A workshop that had been established in the 1950s was extended in the 1980s

to include a scientific and technological restoration department. These not only carried forward the traditions of craftsmanship, but also drew upon the discoveries of natural science to help with the restoration of damaged relics and artifacts. Gradually, the missing valuables are being restored and repaired.

Nowadays, inside the Forbidden City are more than ten museums and the Wen Hua Hall stores more than 10 million official documents drawn up over 500 years by central and local governments of the Ming and Qing dynasties. They are the largest and most valuable collection of historical records in China. The Imperial Library keeps the Si Ku Quan Shu; a 79,337-volume compendium of historical records collected over ten years by China's most accomplished scholars. It all builds up a picture of how the Forbidden City looked and how it was run each day.

SUPERSTITION

Chapter 1 explains why the roofs in the Forbidden City are different colours. Since yellow is the symbol of the royal family, it was the dominant colour of the Forbidden City. Most roofs were built with yellow tiles, many decorations in the palaces were painted yellow and even bricks on the ground were made yellow by a special process. Still, a few palace buildings had black or green tiles instead of yellow. For instance, there were three palace buildings behind the palaces of the emperors' wives which were built with green tiles. These were the residences of the Qing princes. According to superstition, only green tiles could be used for the Qing high-ranking nobles, such as

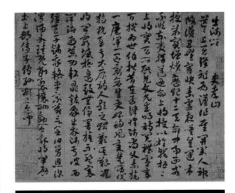

Written documents held at the museum, such as the 'Ode to Dispatching Troops' above is of great historic and artistic value today.

princes, but yellow – the colour of the Sun – could not be used and was only allowed for the emperor himself. On the other hand, the Wenyuan Pavilion, or the royal library, was built with black tiles. According to the ancient Chinese belief, black symbolically represents water (see p. 9). Since the pavilion was used for storing books, it was a fire risk. Therefore, in line with the superstitious idea of the ancients, black tiles, meaning water, were used to counteract this. Purple and red were also imperial colours and many of the decorations inside the palaces are in those colours.

Tourists can see a small-scale version of the Forbidden City at the Imperial Palace Museum.

Tales & customs – THE FIVE ELEMENTS

The layout of the Forbidden City is rectangular, but the planning is circular, in accordance to Chinese beliefs of the Five Elements:

1. *Wood burns producing fire;*

2. *Fire leaves behind earth;*

3. *Earth is the source of metal;*

4. *Metal liquifies into flowing liquid like water;*

5. *Water then becomes the nourishment of the wood.*

THE NINE DRAGON SCREEN

Animals and numbers were also symbolic to the people of China during the Ming and Qing dynasties. Behind the Hall of Preserved Harmony, in the middle of the stairway, is the 'Nine Dragon Screen'. This is the biggest stone sculpture in the Forbidden high and about 30 metres long. Made up of 270 tiles, it shows nine dragons playing with pearls against a background of the sea and clouds. The screen is coloured in shades of yellow, blue, white and violet. The number of dragons symbolises the supreme importance of the emperor. Nine is the highest single number, while represents the emperor as the Son of Heaven. The belly of the third white dragon has a piece of wood sticking out of it. It is said that the dragon broke when it was being made. This would have meant that the craftsman making it would have been punished with death had his mistake been discovered, so a carpenter repaired

The Nine Dragon Screen is the biggest stone sculpture at the Forbidden City. As was the case with most animal sculptures, dragons were symbolic to the Chinese people. Among other things, the dragons were the specific symbol of the royal family.

City. Anyone who was caught touching this holy stone would be punished by death. One of three such screens built in China, the Nine Dragon Screen at the Forbidden City is the largest. Built in 1771 during the reign of Emperor Qianlong, it is 3.5 metres five is in the middle, between one and nine. So the screen has nine dragons with five further dragons on the border. The Chinese dragon represented heaven and the power of man as well as being the emblem of the imperial family. So the Nine Dragon Screen it with a piece of wood to keep the damage from being spotted by the emperor's inspector!

MAN-MADE HILL

Overlooking the Forbidden City is a man-made hill using the earth taken from excavations of the

climbed up the hill and prayed for an uneventful year. The hill was called Coal Hill and it is believed that a hidden coal supply was buried there for the imperial family. It was on this hill that the last Ming emperor, Congzhen, hanged himself.

MING TOMBS

About 40 kilometres northwest of Beijing, the Ming emperors were buried in tombs. The Ming Tombs cover an area of over 40 kilometres in circumference and thirteen of the 16 emperors of the Ming dynasty (1368–1644) were buried there. At the gate to the tomb area stands a marble archway, which leads to the Sacred or Spirit Way. Large stone animal statues line both sides of this, including a giant tortoise-like animal. Excavations of the Ming Tombs have, over the years, uncovered many rare treasures, such as the gold royal crowns and the silk robes that the emperors used to wear.

imperial moat in 1420. According to ancient Chinese beliefs, this hill would protect the Forbidden City from any evil spirits swooping in from the north, which bring only death and misery, according to Feng Shui. Emperor Yongle ordered that flowers and trees be planted there and cranes and deer be raised there. Every year on the ninth day of the ninth month, he

Looking south from Coal Hill in Jingshan Park provides a clear view of the Forbidden City.

This ceremonial robe would have been worn by Emperor Qianlong and is currently on show at the museum.

A day in the life

For the 500 years that the Ming and Qing emperors ruled there, no one was allowed inside the Forbidden City except the emperor's family and officials. Nowadays it is a public museum, (since 1925) and a world heritage site (since 1987). Every day crowds of people pass through the Meridian Gate that used to be the emperor's entrance, the Gate of Spiritual Valour in the north, or either of the two smaller gates to the east and west, to explore and wonder at the magnificent architecture, statues, furnishings and over one million artifacts and tranquil gardens.

VISITING THE CITY

Now open to everyone, the Forbidden City remains a symbol of Chinese rule and imperial power. It is a timeless example of ancient Chinese architecture and of the principles of Feng Shui. Certain buildings within the city take it in turns to display art collections and house temporary exhibitions. The most precious items are exhibited in the Palace of Peaceful Longevity. Every year the 600 year old Palace Museum receives between six to eight million visitors from all over the world, but mainly people from China. People who work there today have vastly different job descriptions to the workers from the Ming and Qing dynasties. Workers today keep the place clean and in good repair, they take visitors on guided tours, work in the shops and cafés, and they guard the valuable buildings and works of art. As well as guides, cleaners and security guards, many more people work in the various offices that have been set up within the city, including the department of antiquities, the department of paintings and calligraphy, the palace department and the exhibition, promotion and education department.

Where it was once a private and desolate place, today the Forbidden City is densely populated with local and visiting people.

Visitors can enjoy the city in various ways. Before actually reaching the Meridian Gate, there are several restaurants and a market outside, near Tiananmen Square. Then, at the City gates, people can stroll about, walking into the rooms and halls that are on display at their own leisure or join a guided tour.

A group of Sumo wrestlers at the Forbidden City take a moment to relax.

Today, in the Hall of Preserving Harmony in the Outer Court, there is a café for everyone to enjoy. Years ago, this Hall was only used by emperors and nobles for feasts on the evening of the Chinese New Year. The café today is busy, but tastefully decorated, with no big signs or anything that detracts from the site's atmosphere or the artefacts and original decorations around the walls and ceiling. Within the City are seven galleries, including the Pottery Gallery, the Clock Gallery, the Treasure Gallery and the Jade Gallery. Each gallery holds artefacts and works of art from the City's rich history.

GIGANTIC PORTRAIT

For a small extra fee, visitors can climb the steps of Tiananmen Gate to look out over the great courtyard and see the panoramic view where emperors inspected their armies or judged prisoners. A gigantic portrait of Chairman Mao has been hanging there since 1949, along with two placards. One reads 'Long live the People's Republic of China' and the other one reads 'Long live the great unity of the world's peoples'. Today on the western side of the Forbidden City, is a group of buildings. These are the central headquarters for the Communist Party of China – a sign that the power of the emperors has gone forever.

A portrait of Chairman Mao hangs over the Gate of Heavenly Peace, the entrance to the City.

Tales & customs – SERVING HEAVEN

The Gate of Supreme Harmony was one of the original buildings of the Ming city. The Ming called it the Gate of Serving Heaven. The Qing renamed it, along with many other buildings, to incorporate and emphasise their commitment to peace and harmony. It was the first working part of the Forbidden City. Protocol demanded that visitors entered the gate through the entrance appropriate for their rank. The gate is an important place where emperors' wedding ceremonies were usually held.

Preserving the past

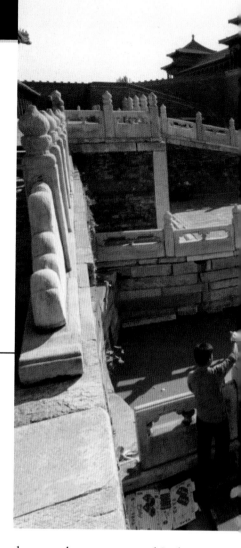

S ince the Forbidden City was first built for Emperor Yongle in 1420, maintenance and repair work has been constant. The exception to this was between the years of 1911 and 1948 when social conditions, such as the downfall of the Qing dynasty and the two world wars, prevented it and the city fell into disrepair. Restoration and repair work has continued to take place from the 1950s to the present.

Keeping the City clean was considered a top priority during the Ming and Qing Dynasties and remains the case today.

RETIREMENT RESTORATION

For nearly a century, one of the most opulent structures inside the Forbidden City sat decaying and unseen. It was the Palace of Peaceful Longevity, the retirement home of Emperor Qianlong which he had built between 1771 and 1776. Out of respect for his grandfather, Qianlong chose to step down from the throne after nearly 60 years so as not to rule for longer than Kangxi, who had ruled for 61 years. At the age of 84, Qianlong abdicated in favour of his son Jiaqing and lived happily in this palace, although he secretly continued to be involved in imperial affairs until his death three years later. Originally, this palace contained many richly decorated chambers, including a theatre where Chinese harps, violins and the Beijing opera played. It was surrounded by a four-courtyard garden where Qianlong liked to sit and think in the evenings. To a certain extent, Qianlong had opened up China to the Western world and this is reflected in the objects he used in the lodge – a mixture of Qing dynasty decorations and Italian paintings, which he greatly admired. The walls and ceilings were adorned with ornate wood carvings, jade, embroideries and large paintings created by the Italian Jesuit missionary, Giuseppe Castiglione. Now a massive restoration project is set to return the palace to its former glory. But restorations are not always straightforward. For instance, some of the same ancient materials are no longer available and specialists of certain techniques cannot always be found or learn skills easily. These are problems that even modern technology cannot resolve.

Specialists are employed to restore delicate porcelain treasures.

A SYMBOL OF CHINESE HISTORY

In the early 1950s, great efforts were made to return the city to the magnificent and awe-inspiring place it had once been. Dirty and dilapidated halls and courts, that

Many workers are employed at the Forbidden City to attend to the constant repairs and maintenance required to preserve the City's original magnificence.

lay under weeds and piles of rubbish, were cleared and cleaned. Crumbling walls were repaired and redecorated, and all buildings

were fixed up with lighting, fire protection and security alarms. The moat, or Outer and Inner Golden Water was dredged and cleaned. The Forbidden City is still the biggest complex of palaces in the world and is considered by the Chinese government to be one of the most important historical monuments in the country. Now, the Forbidden City, or Palace Museum as it is called today, has been put under special preservation. This means that there is a constant programme of repair and restoration to the buildings, aimed

Tales & customs – THE JADE DOCUMENT

One other ceremony that took place inside the Hall of Central Harmony was the updating and presentation to the Emperor of the Qing family tree, the Jade Document. Three copies were made of the document: one to be housed in the Imperial Archives within the Forbidden City, one for the Clan Register Office in Beijing and one for the Old Palace in Shenyang – the original centre of Manchu power.

The Forbidden City

at bringing them back into the condition they were in when the emperors lived and ruled there. Almost every day, experts work on some area of the city, bringing it back to its former glory for the visitors from around the world to come and marvel at.

In the early 1980s, the Meridian Gate and some of the great ceremonial halls were restored. Several apartments were refurbished to their 19th century state, while others were returned to the appearance they had during earlier periods. The renovations

Many run-down houses near the Forbidden City in Beijing are being demolished and rebuilt as part of a plan to 'preserve' historic sites. All historic sites and cultural relics are protected throughout the process.

are extremely expensive and need the skills of many architects, historians, scientists and other experts, but this is considered vital in order to allow people to see and appreciate the past in all its splendour. Computers are being used to show how the buildings and interiors used to look and could still look when restored. The repairs will also help to revive and restore some ancient skills

Tales & customs – BEIJING OPERA

The Beijing opera was often performed for the Emperor. It consisted of the 'internal troupe', which was made up of eunuchs and the 'external troupe' whose actors were specially selected to come and perform to the Emperor and his family. The Beijing opera is a unique form of opera, combining dance, acrobatics and music. The costumes, make-up and gestures all have symbolic meanings, which audiences of imperial China would have understood and been familiar with.

The Imperial Seals, held in the Hall of Union, are wrapped in plastic to protect them from damage.

arrival at the City and the costumes of the imperial court: 'The imposing Gate of Spiritual Valour, through which I made my first entrance into the Forbidden City on March 3, 1919, led me to a new world of space and time ... on the inner side of the gateway were to be observed palanquins bearing stately mandarins with ruby and coral 'buttons' and peacocks' feathers on their official hats and white cranes and golden pheasants on the front of their long outer garments of silk.'

Although the Forbidden City has undergone many transformations throughout the centuries, stepping into the vast Outer Court is like stepping back several centuries into imperial China as it once was. Emperor Yongle might have been pleased to see that it remains an amazing symbol of the rich history of China – for all to see.

and techniques that were practised by the artists and craftspeople of imperial China, which were being lost in time. There is now a reason for some of the skills and techniques to be used, but training people and paying for their expertise is costly.

SEEING THROUGH TWILIGHT

The British official, scholar and writer, Reginald F. Johnson (1874–1938) served as tutor and moral advisor to Puyi, the last emperor of China. He wrote about his experiences in a book that was published in 1934, called *Twilight in the Forbidden City*. Through the vivid descriptions in this book about his life and surroundings in th Forbidden City, experts have been able to restore and renovate many of the decorations and buildings to their former appearance. In the following excerpt, he describes his

Temporary scaffolding is erected over one of the Forbidden City palaces in order for it to be renovated.

Glossary

Abdicated Gave up the role of king or queen to make way for another to take the throne.

Ancestors Family who lived before us, whom we have descended from.

Anglo-Palladian An 18th century architectural style combining the technique of 16th century Italian architect Andrea Palladio with English architectural styles.

Artefacts An object produced or shaped by human craft, especially a tool, weapon, or ornament of historical interest.

Autocratic Ruled by one leader who holds all the power over the country or state.

Balustrades Ornamental railings or pillars of a building.

Buddhism The teaching of Buddha that life is full of suffering caused by desire, that suffering ceases when desire ceases, and that enlightenment obtained through wisdom and meditation releases one from desire and suffering.

Calligraphy Beautiful handwriting that is an art form. The technique takes many years to master.

Communism When all property is publicly owned and everyone is paid and works according to their needs.

Concubine A woman who lives with a man without being married to him.

Contemplation Thoughtful observation or study.

Corruption Dishonest or illegal behaviour.

Counterfeiting The act of forging or imitating something.

Courtiers Companions and advisors to the ruler of a nation.

Crane A long-necked bird.

Daoism Philosophical system that believes in living a simple, honest life and not interfering with the natural course of events.

Dowager An elderly woman of high social station who holds a title or property derived from her deceased husband.

Dynasty A succession of rulers belonging to the same family.

Emasculated Surgically removed male testicles.

Emperor The name for the male ruler of an empire.

Enamel A glass-like or semi-transparent hard coating applied to glass, pottery and metal objects.

Eunuch A male servant who is castrated. Half of all eunuchs died after the operation took place.

Exorcism Driving out an evil spirit.

Famine Food shortage.

Feng Shui The Chinese belief that by positioning objects (such as buildings and furniture) in a way that is harmonious with patterns of 'yin' and 'yang' and the flow of 'chi', an increased amount of happiness and good things will result.

Humidity Amount of moisture in the atmosphere.

Imperial Describes something under the Empire rule. As 'royal' is to kings and queens, 'imperial' is to emperors and empresses.

Incense A substance that is burned for the sweet smell it produces.

Jesuit Member of the Society of Jesus, a Roman Catholic order of priests.

Longevity Long life.

Manchu A member of a people native to Manchuria, who ruled China during the Qing dynasty.

Ming A Chinese dynasty (1368–1644) noted for its foreign trade, achievements in scholarship and development of the arts, especially in porcelain, textiles and painting.

Missionary A person who travels to spread the word about his or her faith.

Moat The body of water usually surrounding a castle or tower.

Mongol A member of the traditionally nomadic (travelling) peoples of Mongolia.

Movable type A method of printing using raised letters that fit into grooves, which are inked on and printed. Each letter can be moved around to create different words.

Nationalism Beliefs held by people within a country, based on that country's identity.

Nobility Aristocracy, upper class.

Officials People who have jobs in the government.

Omens Things that are believed to be signs of good or evil events to come.

Opulent Possessing or showing great wealth.

Pawned An object lent in return for an amount of money.

Peking The name given to the capital of China by French missionaries 400 years ago. The name was changed back to its correct name of Beijing in 1949 by the Communist Party of China.

Philosophy The study of knowledge, reality and existence.

Phoenix A mythical bird that died in a burst of flames then rose again to life from the ashes.

Pole Star A star located in the sky directly above the North Pole.

Porcelain A light, smooth form of delicate white clay used to make ornaments and crockery such as plates and bowls.

Portico A porch or walkway with a roof supported by columns, often leading to the entrance of a building.

Prosperity Success or good fortune.

Prostrate Lie face down.

Protocol Official behaviour or procedure.

Qianlong Chinese emperor (1735–1796) of the Qing dynasty who subdued the Turkish and Mongolian threats to northern China, expanded the empire and was a patron of the arts.

Qing A Chinese dynasty (1644–1912) during which Western influence and trade led to the Opium War (1839–1842) with Britain and the Boxer Rebellion (1898–1900). The dynasty, China's last, was overthrown by nationalist revolutionaries.

Regent Person appointed to lead a nation because the monarch is too young or unfit to rule.

Relics Objects or beliefs from an earlier time.

Republic State in which power is held by the people.

Revolution The overthrow of a government by force.

Scholar An academic person.

Tranquillity Peaceful, free from disturbances.

Tyrant Bully or oppressor.

Valour Courage in the face of danger.

Yin & Yang Chinese philosophy linked to Feng Shui, related to balance and harmony. Yin is the female, softer aspect of the world and yang is the masculine, stronger aspect of the world. A balance of a certain amount of both yin and yang is needed in everything.

Yuan Chinese dynasty (1279–1368) established by the Mongolian ruler Kublai Khan.

Index

Copyright © ticktock Entertainment Ltd 2005
First published in Great Britain in 2005 by ticktock Media Ltd.,
Unit 2, Orchard Business Centre, North Farm Road, Tunbridge Wells, Kent, TN2 3XF
We would like to thank: Alison Howard, Elizabeth Wiggans and Jenni Rainford for their help with this book.
Printed in China. A CIP catalogue record for this book is available from the British Library.

Picture Credits
AA World Travel Library: 2–3, 4L; Associated Press: 39B, 40, 41L, 44L, 45R; Art Archive: 6L, 10, 11L, 12L, 13B, 14L, 14R, 16–17, 27R, 31L, 32L, 33R,
36L, 37R; Bridgeman Art Library: 6–7, 11R, 15, 20B, 21B, 26L, 26–27, 28–29, 31R, 32–33; Corbis: 4–5, 7R, 9T, 16L, 17R, 18T, 18B, 19T, 20–21, 21R,
22L, 22R, 23B, 24L, 24–25, 25BL, 25R, 28, 29R, 30, 34, 35B, 36–37, 38–39, 39T, 41R, 43R, 44–45; Getty Images: 35T; Heritage Images: 5R; Reuters:
42L, 42–43; Robert Harding Picture Library: 18–19; Werner Forman Archives: 8L, 9B, 12–13, 23T